Fiscal Responsibility
Tax Increases
or Spending Cuts?

THE CHARLES C. MOSKOWITZ LECTURES NUMBER XIV

Paul McCracken

EDMUND EZRA DAY UNIVERSITY PROFESSOR OF
BUSINESS ADMINISTRATION
UNIVERSITY OF MICHIGAN

Murray L. Weidenbavm

EDWARD MALLINCKRODT DISTINGUISHED
UNIVERSITY PROFESSOR
WASHINGTON UNIVERSITY

Lawrence S. Ritter

PROFESSOR OF FINANCE
NEW YORK UNIVERSITY

Robert A. Kavesh

PROFESSOR OF FINANCE
NEW YORK UNIVERSITY

Fiscal Responsibility
Tax Increases
or Spending Cuts?

CHARLES C. MOSKOWITZ LECTURES
SCHOOL OF COMMERCE
NEW YORK UNIVERSITY

NEW YORK   *New York University Press*

1973

LONDON   *University of London Press*

238685

FOREWORD

The Charles C. Moskowitz Lectures are arranged by the College of Business and Public Administration of New York University and aim at advancing public understanding of the issues that are of major concern to business and the nation. Established through the generosity of Mr. Charles C. Moskowitz, a distinguished alumnus of the College and a former Vice President-Treasurer and Director of Loew's Inc., they have enabled the College to make a significant contribution to public discussion and understanding of important issues facing the American economy and its business enterprises.

The fourteenth in the series of Charles C. Moskowitz Lectures was planned to focus on the topic "Fiscal Responsibility: Tax Increases or Spending Cuts?" and provided a forum for four distinguished economists to discuss that question. Paul W. McCracken, former Chairman of the Council of Economic Advisers and now Edmund Day University Professor of Business Administration at the University of Michigan, presented a paper on "Foundations for Economic Policy in the 1970s," while Murray L. Weidenbaum, former Assistant Secretary of the Treasury and now Mallinckrodt Distinguished University Professor at Washington University, lectured on "Government Expenditures and National Priorities." Comments on the two lectures were then made by Professors Robert Kavesh and Lawrence Ritter of the Faculty of Business Administration of New York University.

Once again, the Charles C. Moskowitz Lectures achieved their purpose, for they engendered significant and provocative papers by the lecturers and critical yet constructive comments by the discussants. A reading of this volume will quickly disclose the sharpness of some of the differences which emerged. But it will be rewarding, for it will encourage independent thinking on a subject which is ineluctably interrelated with such vital contemporary issues as inflation, national objectives and priorities, congressional ability (or inability) to control expenditures, the balance of payments, and so on.

As always, Mrs. Patricia Matthias, my administrative assistant, and Mrs. Katherine Lopez, my secretary, were responsible for the many details connected with the lectures, and I express my appreciation to them. I express appreciation also to the staff of the New York University Press.

Abraham L. Gitlow
Dean
College of Business and
   Public Administration
New York University

June 1973

THE CHARLES C. MOSKOWITZ LEC-
TURES were established through the generosity
of a distinguished alumnus of the College of Business and Public Administration, Mr. Charles C.
Moskowitz of the Class of 1914, who retired after
many years as Vice President-Treasurer and
a Director of Loew's Inc.

In establishing these lectures, it was Mr.
Moskowitz's aim to contribute to the understanding of the function of business and its underlying
disciplines in society by providing a public forum
for the dissemination of enlightened business
theories and practices.

The College of Business and Public Administration and New York University are deeply
grateful to Mr. Moskowitz for his continued interest in, and contribution to, the educational and
public service program of his alma mater.

This volume is the fourteenth in the Moskowitz series. The earlier ones were:

February, 1961 *Business Survival in the Sixties*
Thomas F. Patton, President and Chief Executive Officer
Republic Steel Corporation

November, 1961 *The Challenges Facing Management*
Don G. Mitchell, President
General Telephone and Electronics Corporation

November, 1962 *Competitive Private Enterprise Under Government Regulation*
Malcolm A. MacIntyre, President
Eastern Air Lines

November, 1963 *The Common Market: Friend or Competitor?*
Jesse W. Markham, Professor of Economics, Princeton University
Charles E. Fiero, Vice President, The Chase Manhattan Bank
Howard S. Piquet, Senior Specialist in International Economics, Legislative Reference Service, The Library of Congress

November, 1964 *The Forces Influencing the American Economy*
Jules Backman, Research Professor of Economics, New York University

Martin R. Gainsbrugh, Chief Economist and Vice President, National Industrial Conference Board

November, 1965 *The American Market of the Future*
Arno H. Johnson, Vice President and Senior Economist, J. Walter Thompson Company
Gilbert E. Jones, President, IBM World Trade Corporation
Darrell B. Lucas, Professor of Marketing and Chairman of the Department, New York University

November, 1966 *Government Wage-Price Guideposts in the American Economy*
George Meany, President, American Federation of Labor and Congress of Industrial Organizations
Roger M. Blough, Chairman of the Board and Chief Executive Officer, United States Steel Corporation
Neil H. Jacoby, Dean, Graduate School of Business Administration, University of California at Los Angeles

November, 1967 *The Defense Sector in the American Economy*

14

Jacob K. Javits, United States Senator, New York
Charles J. Hitch, President, University of California
Arthur F. Burns, Chairman, Federal Reserve Board

November, 1968 The Urban Environment: How It Can Be Improved
William E. Zisch, Vice-chairman of the Board, Aerojet-General Corporation
Paul H. Douglas, Chairman, National Commission on Urban Problems
Professor of Economics, New School for Social Research
Robert C. Weaver, President, Bernard M. Baruch College of the City University of New York
Former Secretary of Housing and Urban Development

November, 1969 Inflation: The Problems It Creates and the Policies It Requires
Arthur M. Okun, Senior Fellow, The Brookings Institution
Henry H. Fowler, General Partner, Goldman, Sachs & Co.
Milton Gilbert, Economic Adviser, Bank for International Settlements

March, 1971   *The Economics of Pollution*
Kenneth E. Boulding, Professor of Economics, University of Colorado
Elvis J. Stahr, President, National Audubon Society
Solomon Fabricant, Professor of Economics, New York University
Former Director, National Bureau of Economic Research
Martin R. Gainsbrugh, Adjunct Professor of Economics, New York University
Chief Economist, National Industrial Conference Board

April, 1971   *Young America in the NOW World*
Hubert H. Humphrey, Senator from Minnesota
Former Vice President of the United States

April, 1972   *Optimum Social Welfare and Productivity: A Comparative View*
Jan Tinbergen, Professor of Development Planning, Netherlands School of Economics

16

CONTENTS

19

FOUNDATIONS FOR ECONOMIC POLICY IN THE 1970s

Paul W. McCracken

Edmund Ezra Day University
Professor of Business Administration
The University of Michigan

At the time that this invitation was extended, I had expected to have some thoughts ready about the impact of our tax system on the economy and more broadly (since I pose as no technical expert on tax matters) the role of the budget in the management of economic policy. There are some comments on these matters in this paper, but in the light of developments during the last year or so I found the paper taking shape within a much broader framework than had been anticipated earlier. For events have been moving fast in recent months, and it is not amiss for us to evaluate their significance as we examine the tools which the managers of economic policy must use in trying to attain their objectives.

I

This seems appropriate because the economies of the industrial world are at a crossroad. If the right course is taken, the 1970's may yet go into the annals of history as one in which material levels of living and employment moved upward on a sustained basis and within the framework of an international economy of growing liberality and interdependence. If the wrong turn in the road is taken, we could find ourselves moving along a course of stop-go domestic production and employment and rapidly mounting restrictions that would impede economic progress, court the risk of political disorder, and even put in jeopardy our fundamentally liberal social order.

That the stakes are heavy in the choices that are now being made is clear enough for those with some sense of historical perspective. And it is well for all of us to recall Santayana's warning:

Those who cannot remember the past
are condemned to repeat it.

During the interlude between World Wars I and II, after 200 years of enormous progress toward realizing the dividends of growing international economic interdependence, we got ourselves 180 degrees off course. The consequences were political and economic disasters. By the outbreak of World War II manufacturing output in the industrial world was roughly double that on the eve of World War I, but world trade in manufactured products was actually below the level prevailing in that earlier period. The consequences of this autarky for an inefficient utilization of the world's productive resources were self-evident, but these moves toward self-sufficiency, difficult to reverse when once set in motion, also exacerbated the cumulating international political tensions.

It requires no misanthropic pessimist to see in the world economy today some profoundly disturbing developments. The one that has been most on our minds has been the international monetary crisis that brought to an end the Smithsonian agreement, itself requiring great labor pains to see the light of day, after just over one year. Anyone traveling abroad frequently, as I do, is painfully aware of the fact that the D-mark or 100-yen coin, somewhat smaller than a U.S. quarter, now cost Americans close to 40 cents instead of 28 cents as recently as mid-1971; and with no unseemly eagerness on the part of the market to make many transactions even at that rate.

These monetary disturbances are, however, the symptoms of our problem rather than their substance. They are, to invoke the economist's phrase used in another connection, the thermometer registering the heat rather than the furnace producing it. An examination of the broad mosaic of international trade patterns makes it clear that all has not been well in the world of trade and commerce for some time. The most profound change has been the declining U.S. share of exports to the industrial countries, and the explosive rise in the share accounted for by Japan. From 25 percent in 1964, the year of our largest trade surplus during the 1960's, the U.S. share dropped to just over 18 percent in 1972. Japan's share by contrast almost doubled during that period, rising from 6 percent in 1964 to something like 11 percent last year, and Germany's share also rose about two percentage points during that period.

Now the fact that shares of the world's exports show substantial changes among industrial nations is itself no cause for concern, though such facts may be useful in any sermon to the laggard economies about getting with it. When we look at the import side of the picture, however, we do begin to see a problem. The U.S. last year accounted for about 21½ percent of the industrial countries' total imports, substantially larger than its 18½ percent share of 1964. And during that same period Japan's share of these imports rose only from about 7 percent in 1964 to about 8¾ percent last year—a gain of less than two percentage points, while its share of these countries' exports rose by more than five percentage points. And Germany's share of total imports rose about one percentage point, compared with a 2 point gain in its share of exports. These disparate changes have, of course, brought us to a pattern of trade that cannot be sustained, though the therapy apparently preferred by others is for the U.S. to restore balance in its trade account in ways that would involve no reduction of exports by each other country to us and no increase in our exports to each of them in turn.

The problem is that we now have vested-interest export industries in surplus nations that, like any vested interest, resist policies threatening what has been a relatively favored position. This has made it politically difficult for surplus nations, particularly for Japan, to take measures needed to correct a trade surplus of serious proportions. And it has led Germany to an expansion of its industrial structure that out-paced its indigenous labor force, with the result that the country now faces difficult social and political problems because roughly 10 percent of its work force is there "temporarily" from other nations. And we also have domestic vested interests in other countries prodding governments toward protectionist measures. We are acutely aware of that here, but we also see manifestations of it elsewhere. More recently a new brand of trade restrictions has emerged in the form of growing export controls as governments respond to domestic pressures incident to intense world demands for products ranging from oil to logs and soy beans.

When we turn from developments in external trade to conditions within domestic economies, we also find some serious disequilibria. For one thing, the rate of inflation is high and rising. The median rate of rise in the consumer price index for countries in the industrial world during the last 12 months for which data are available was about 7 percent, and such solid and politically stable countries as Switzerland, Germany, and the United Kingdom are in that zone. Moreover, in its December review of the economic outlook the O.E.C.D. found little to indicate any significant improvement in prospects for the price level. For the O.E.C.D. countries as a whole, in fact, the projection is for a somewhat more rapid rise in the price level from 1972 to 1973 than from 1971 to 1972. And developments since the end of the year for world food prices suggest that even the

O.E.C.D.'s projections may themselves be too sanguine.

These prospects for inflation are all the more troublesome because they are emerging at a time when there has been persistent slack in many economies of the industrial world. Legitimate questions can be raised—indeed, need to be raised —about the reliability of these "gap" estimates as guides for economic policy. In the United States, for example, the pursuit of highly expansive policies until the gap as conventionally measured disappears would almost certainly set off a sharp acceleration in the price level generally. Even so we do have to recognize that in economies representing two-thirds to three quarters of the industrial world, there is a good deal of evidence that operating rates have been somewhat below comfortably full utilization of productive resources. These gaps have been particularly visible for Italy and Japan, but they have existed in varying degrees also for Canada, the U.K., the U.S., and for certain smaller countries such as Australia.

In the domestic scene, therefore, the managers of economic policy continue to confront the problem that has been so vexatious during the last decade—namely, a tendency for the rate of inflation to accelerate before full employment, at least as conventionally defined, has been reached. And some of these nations (e.g., the U.K. and the U.S.) have found themselves with a weak external payments problem even as unemployment persisted and an accelerating rate of inflation threatened.

II

Since we here after all have a particular stake in the performance of the U.S. economy, a few quick comments about policy during recent years may be in order. Perhaps the fiscal policy that we had after 1965 should not have been pursued; but it was, the result was a seriously overheated economy and an accelerating inflation had to be countered. It had to be countered because things were not working out well for any broad group in the economy. Real spendable income per working family showed no gains after 1965, and real corporate profits were declining. Moreover these strains were opening up serious fissures among groups in our society, each assuming that since it was doing badly others must be waxing fat. Businessmen became almost obsessive about the problems of wage-cost inflation, and labor costs per unit of output were rising rapidly. Union leaders, however, found themselves negotiating for new contracts against the back drop of no gains or even losses in the real take home pay of their members. And the inflation and the inflationmindedness had also completely distorted judgments about values in financial management for businesses.

In economic policy it is not easy at times to distinguish between success and failure. Expansion is good and comfortable and, unless egregiously overdone as after 1965, it is apt to be declared a success. Disinflation is always painful and is not apt to get high marks even if reasonably successful. The basic strategy for dealing with this complex problem was straightforward. First, general demand pressures on the economy had to be relieved through a shift of fiscal and monetary restraint. The resulting shift in fiscal policy was of dramatic proportions.

EXPANSIVE THRUST OF FISCAL POLICY
(Unified budget in billions)

Fiscal Year	Increase In Outlays (—)	Revenue from Tax Rate Increases (=)	Fiscal Thrust
1968	$20.5	$—4.2	$24.7
1969	5.8	17.0	—11.2
1970	12.2	—0.2	12.4
1971	14.8	—7.4	22.2
1972	20.5	—8.2	28.7

Source: Basic data from the Budget Messages.

We need an unambiguous measure of the expansiveness of fiscal policy—of the influence that the aggregate of the Federal government's fiscal operations exerts on the volume of economic activity. The most conventional measure is probably the size of the deficit, but clearly this will not do. A large deficit can be a reflection of rapid economic expansion if, for example, Federal spending jumps as in fiscal years 1966-1968; or it can be a reflection of economic decline with its resulting short-fall of revenues as in 1970 and 1971. A figure for the deficit leaves us with no way of knowing whether it reflects economic strength or economic weakness. There is, however, a reasonably unambiguous measure of the extent to which, apart from other influences, the fiscal operations of government would increase the level of economic activity. An increase in the level of Federal spending, other things being equal, will tend to increase the demand for output, and an increase in tax rates will tend to reduce private demand because after-tax incomes would be lowered. The first minus the second is, therefore, a crude but reasonably unambiguous calibration of fiscal policy (recognizing that either term can be plus or minus).

Thus measured, the magnitude of the fiscal thrust shifted from +$24.7 billion to a −$11.2 billion from FY 1968 to FY 1969. This is probably a leading candidate for the most activist fiscal policy of recent decades. It was partly the tax increase in June 1968, but it also reflected the Draconian measures taken early in calendar 1969 to curb spending. The result was a small $5.8 billion increase in outlays from FY 1968 to FY 1969 compared with a $20.5 billion increase in the prior year. Fiscal policy after FY 1969 then became progressively more expansive, with this measure of fiscal thrust or push rising to $28.7 billion in FY 1972.

The record of fiscal policy during this period has been reviewed in some detail here for two reasons. One is to dispel any misapprehensions about whether fiscal policy was "passive" in these years. The empirical evidence is quite clear that it was a vigorous exercise in fiscal management. The second reason is more fundamental. We had here a real world demonstration that fiscal policy can be managed in a reasonably timely way if there is the will to deflect the trend of outlays. We are not inexorably prisoners of fiscal viscosities when there is the will to change direction.

Monetary policy broadly complemented fiscal policy during these years. After a rapid rate of expansion during 1968, particularly from October 1968 to February 1969, the monetary brakes went on in early 1969, with policy particularly severe after mid-year. Indeed, from July to December that year the money supply rose at the rate of only 1.2 percent per year. Shortly after the turn

of the year into 1970, monetary expansion was
again resumed.

RATE OF EXPANSION OF THE MONEY STOCK

Period	Rate
12/67-12/68	7.8%
12/68-12/69	3.6
12/69-12/70	6.0
12/70-12/71	6.7

Source: Basic data from the Federal Reserve.

That the strategy worked is now a matter of
history. The rate of inflation reached its crest of
roughly 7 percent per year rate early in 1970 and
began to settle to lower levels. The unemployment rate rose, but this had to be expected, and
as Chairman-designate of the Council of Economic Advisers I warned in my early press inter-
views that this could not be avoided. Even so,
the unemployment rate rose to a level only 1½
percentage points above that consistent with
reasonably full employment.

The foundation was thereby laid for the re-
sumption of strong and orderly expansion of production and employment with a price level performance that compared favorably with that for

the industrial world generally. Indeed, the rate of inflation was the lowest during 1972 of the major industrial nations, and the rise in industrial output was the largest except for that of Japan.

CHANGE IN PRODUCTION AND THE PRICE
LEVEL, 1972

Country	Industrial Production	Consumer Price Index
Canada	7.5%	5.1%
France	—12.9	6.8
Germany	7.6	6.4
Italy	4.8	7.2
Japan	12.5	4.8
U.K.	5.6	7.7
U.S.	10.3	3.5

Source: *International Financial Statistics,* May 1973. Figures are the change from the fourth quarter of 1971 to the fourth quarter of 1972.

III

What will now be required if we are to make out of the present vigorous economy an enduring expansion? First, we must be realistic here about how high we can push the proportion of the labor force that is employed before the economy starts to manifest many of the symptoms of full employment. Here we are courting danger in the management of economic policy by relying too exclusively on the single statistic of the unemployment rate in judging the remaining slack to be taken up. This slack is a complex thing. Fortunately we now have several measures of internal pressures that may be building up in the economy. We know that delivery schedules have been lengthening rapidly, that a growing proportion of firms report a need for more capacity, that raw materials markets have been reflecting mounting pressures, and that the index of help-wanted advertising has risen sharply. These suggest the need for a slower rate of expansion even though the unemployment rate is still 5 percent. As the economy's operating rate moves into the higher zone, pushing the employment rate higher shifts to the more complex task of getting people with inadequate skills or the wrong location, who generally are at the outer margin of employability, into productive employment at a wage commensurate with their productivity. This remains an urgent social question, but it is a different problem from generally inadequate demand.

Since the internal cumulative forces of expansion are now beginning to build, monetary and fiscal policy must both be less expansive. This seems to be emerging, though the timing is uncomfortably close. One of the most difficult problems for the managers of economic policy is to make the right decision about timing. The visible effects of policy changes show up in the economy only after an interval of substantial but uncertain length. How much longer an expansion needs to run before capacity will be crowded cannot be estimated with precision. Clearly if expansive policies are not moderated until full-employment is regained the lagged effects of these policies will continue for several months and are apt to set off inflation.

Two key questions remain about monetary policy. One is whether we can avoid having a shift toward restraint, once underway, overshoot and give us excessive monetary dehydration. Here the evidence is encouraging. The rate has been brought from the 8 percent pace of 1972 to the 4-6 percent zone, but with monetary expansion continuing. Whether the Federal Reserve will be or feel under excessive pressure, in this era of income policies, to hold interest rates at levels below those consistent with the monetary restraint is another matter of concern. Will, in short, the Federal Reserve be trapped in a "conflict of interest" between what it should do to succeed as the central bank and what would seem to be success in its responsibilities for the level of interest rates and dividends? The citizenry may not be aware of it, but the public interest is very much in the direction of having the central banker function take precedence.

The shape of fiscal policy looks good, except that the timing of the shift is uncomfortably close here also. Because tax rate changes were reductions in FY 1973 and are increases for FY 1974, the fiscal thrust drops from an estimated $23.6 billion this year to an amount projected in this year's Budget Message to be $11.7 billion in FY 1974. This is a sharp decline and one that is very much in order.

FISCAL THRUST, FISCAL YEARS 1973 AND 1974
(Unified budget in billions)

	FY 1973	FY 1974
Projected increase in outlays	$17.9	$18.9
Less: Revenue value, tax rate increases	—5.7	7.2
Total	$23.6	$11.7

Source: Basic data from the Budget Message.

The budget remains highly expansive through FY 1973, and moves toward a less expansive influence only during the first half of FY 1974. If changes in fiscal policy exert their effect on economic conditions with only negligible lags, this fiscal shift will be timed to occur about the time the economy will need to show a decelerating rate of expansion. If there are substantial lags, the fiscal turn wold have been better coming along a half-year earlier.

There is a larger issue of budget policy now emerging. If it comes off reasonably well, it will be the completion of the fiscal revolution that began three or four decades ago. The "new fiscal policy" insisted that the old always-balanced budget philosophy was cyclically perverse. This was correct. The old philosophy seemed to insist that in a recession tax rates must be raised or outlays cut, which would aggravate an already weak economy. And it also meant that tax rates should be reduced or outlays increased in a boom (because budget balance would still permit it). It would be better, the new fiscal policy asserted with quite unexceptionable logic, to recognize that there are times when a budget ought not to be balanced. And this view came to prevail. On the whole the new fiscal policy has performed with reasonable effectiveness in recent years as it endeavored to moderate economic instability. The Administration's failure to go for a tax reduction in 1958 and the delay in the tax increase after 1965 are the major exceptions to this generally favorable judgment, and the sharp perverse shift of the fiscal thrust in 1963 should also be on some such list.

When we replaced the old philosophy with the new, however, we did throw a baby out with the bath water. We threw out the important concept of fiscal discipline. The always-balanced budget philosophy said that if governments responded to the temptation to spend, they must face up to the politically attractive task of levying taxes. Released from this constraint by the logic of the new fiscal policy, the political process has tended to metamorphose from compensatory budget policy to a never-balanced budget philosophy. While, as indicated above, cyclical swings in the budget have generally been phased reasonably well, the budget process with the new fiscal policy has been given an upward secular bias. The figures are dramatic. Since 1965 the rise in government outlays has been equal to more than 50 percent of the rise in national income, and the rise in non-defense outlays has accounted for most of it. That this does not represent the "preferred" allocation of resources is at least strongly suggested by our almost chronic inability to keep the revenue-generating capacity of our tax system, even at reasonably full employment, adequate to cover these outlays.

The first step toward regaining fiscal discipline was the President's insistence that outlays should be held to the revenues the tax system would generate at reasonably full employment. In this way the deficit, which would be proper in a recession, would disappear as the economy returned to full employment. With this rule we began to set some guidelines about outlays, even when stimulus was in order, that would minimize our having then an overly expansive budget during the subsequent expansion.

The next step in the completion of the fiscal revolution occurred last year at the other end of Pennsylvania Avenue with the formation of the Joint Study Committee on Budget Control. The committee seems determined to find a way by which the Congress will make decisions about and accept responsibility for the total. This is obviously essential. Since the aggregate of spending ideas which in each case seems to have merit will always be more than any viable total, the tendency of the present Congressional process to limit itself to screening individual proposals has a logical bias upward. For proper budgetry each item must not only be good but good enough to compete successfully for space within a limited total. In this respect the Federal government's budget problem does parallel that for the family or the business.

The Congress and the public must be patient with initial efforts of the Congress to feel its way toward new procedures for focusing on what total outlays should be, for injecting more of a sense of fiscal discipline into its budgetary process. At the outset these steps will be halting and imperfect, but the effort is essential if we are to regain a more balanced emphasis in the execution of budget policy.

The next important step would be for the President to have limited authority for the variation of tax rates. In this way fiscal policy would gain additional room for maneuver cyclically, and the system of governance would still have the capability to promptly restore balance (or a surplus) to the budget when that became needed. It could be carefully circumscribed to retain ultimate Congressional control. The amount of the change which the President could make should be limited. The President should be required to make a report to the Congress of the findings that led him to propose such action. And there should be provision for a waiting period during which the Congress could veto the President's proposed action.

This will not, of course, soon happen. For obvious reasons the Congress can hardly be expected to take the initiative in giving the President this limited authority over tax rates. What we need is the more vigorous public discussion of this which leads to the acclimatization of public opinion that must occur on any issue before the political process will move. The careful and circumspect nod in this direction by the Council of Economic Advisers in their Annual Report is a lead that the rest of us should follow.

The greatest challenge to economic policy is to find a system that can accommodate in an orderly way a growing volume of trade and commerce within a fundamentally liberal international economy. Here we have come dangerously close to picking up speed going down the road the wrong way. The EEC has lost its outward-looking vision, and sometimes seems to see external trade barriers as the major raison d'être for the club and membership in it. The severe trade imbalances of both Japan and the United States have persisted far too long and were allowed to get far too large. We now see strong and mounting protectionist sentiment at home, and in Germany and Japan powerful vested interests growing out of an overemphasis on exports will make the needed shift in resources difficult for their own political processes to deliver.

In the first version of this address I said:

While the details of any solution will be complex, one point is inescapable. The world will move fairly promptly toward substantially greater flexibility of exchange rates, or it will adopt a mounting array of illiberal direct controls over trade.

Fortunately when governments came to the brink they had the good sense to make the fundamentally right move and choose to operate within the framework of essentially a floating exchange rate system. It is simply inescapable in a dynamic world that competitive positions of economies among themselves will be changing constantly, and these changes must be reflected in exchange rate adjustments or tidal waves of funds will roam around and disequilibrated trading patterns will start to solidify. Finance ministers could all be Solomons in wisdom and saints in intent and still lack the wisdom and virtue to know what pattern of exchange rates would provide balance for the world of early 1972, let alone the different one that would be viable for 1973 or the still different one for 1974. International trade can survive and flourish if traders are having to match their wits against market forces, but it cannot flourish if the system itself caves in on them every year or so.

The U.S. must also give more attention to consultative relationships with those governments whose economies are closely related. The core of such a "group" would obviously be Canada and Japan. Canada is our most important trading partner. Japan is second on that list, and we are her most important trading partner. And Japan is now an affluent and powerful economy with a real per capita GNP well over half that for the U.S. and rising rapidly. In our preoccupation with global matters we have not always been careful in our consultations with this second-largest economy in the Free World. The Japanese are a proud and urbane people, and there is a feeling in Japan that the United States does not give the attention to Japan-U.S. matters that is commensurate with their importance. They have a point. Precisely because the issues in contention between Canada and the U.S. are difficult and complex, we need a strengthening of our basic consultative machinery here also. This is not to suggest a Canada-Japan-U.S. bloc that would be aimed at waging economic warfare against the European Community. It is not in our interest to wind up with a world of economic blocs crunching against each other. What we do need to recognize is the need for machinery that gives expression to the particular importance of Canada and Japan in our economic relationships. Indeed, a by-product of these efforts could well be to draw the European Community back toward the more outward-looking focus that was an inspiring part of its original vision.

V

There are, in short, solid grounds for hope as we look down the road ahead. Monetary policy is now being managed within closer tolerances and in a more timely way. With the new concern about the need for fiscal discipline in our budget procedures, the fiscal revolution that began before World War II may be coming to full fruition. Governments have made decisions that may set the shape of the emergent international economic order in a more powerful and constructive way. While we must not ignore history, we must also avoid having our attitudes shaped by the shadows of developments whose underlying substance has been changed.

GOVERNMENT EXPENDITURES AND NATIONAL PRIORITIES

Murray L. Weidenbaum

Edward Mallinckrodt Distinguished
University Professor
Washington University

It has become fashionable to evoke the phrase "changing our national priorities" in virtually every discussion of public policy in the United States. Certainly there is no lack of attention being given to areas which merit greater priority. Every speaker or writer has his or her favorites—whether it be a cleaner environment or a healthier citizenry or a better educated society.

Yet, despite the difficulties of choice that inevitably arise, identifying the areas to which more resources should be devoted is a relatively simple matter. It is the other side of the coin that is the more difficult and hence is generally ignored—the relatively distasteful or at least unpopular but necessary task of selecting those areas of lower priority to which lesser proportions of our resources should be devoted. I am constantly struck by the one-sidedness of these dicussions on national priorities, particularly when it comes to the subject at hand, that is, fiscal or budget policy.

On reflection we should realize that the process of reordering our priorities is not completed until this vital second step is performed. But—and this of course is the moral of the tale—if we can successfully accomplish this second step, then we may well be able simultaneously to achieve fiscal responsibility and a more responsive set of governmental undertakings, and both without tax increases.

Well, why do we not do that? What are the obstacles that lie in our path? Let me disappoint you at the outset; I neither have a simple diagnosis nor a sure fiscal elixir to offer. Nevertheless, there are several useful and important steps that can be taken to acheive the objectives of greater rationality and effectiveness in government spending. To begin with, we can learn from and build on the efforts of others.

Obstacles to More Effective Decision-Making

Surely, anyone who has researched or worked in this area can quickly enumerate the key obstacles to a more rational allocation of public resources. I will deal with three of them. The first barrier is the presence of numerous fiscal sacred cows or so-called uncontrollable programs which severely inhibit the budget process from the outset. For example, in the fiscal year 1973, less than one-half of the requested appropriations (46 percent is my estimate) were subject to effective review and modification during the entire budget process.[1]

The privileged 54 percent, which is virtually immune from the budgetary scalpel, consists of a host and variety of primarily civilian programs. The largest of these do not even appear in the annual appropriation bills at all—the funds are permanently and automatically appropriated. This is the standard procedure in the case of Social Security benefits, Medicare, interest on the national debt, and unemployment compensation.

For a number of other programs, the annual budget review is perfunctory, a time-consuming but ineffective ritual. Thus, in the case of veterans' pensions, the level of spending is really determined by the number of eligible veterans who apply and qualify for statutorily determined benefits. The budgetary review often is a type of fun and games or "spin the budget." That is, Congress may—after holding extensive appropriation hearings—appropriate less than the amount requested, thus gaining some political advantage for supposedly "cutting" the budget. But when later in the year it is clear that additional funds are needed to carry out the government's legal as well as moral commitment, supplemental appropriations are quickly but quietly voted.

Other examples of these fixed charges or statutory commitments preventing effective budgetary review are found in great abundance— Medicaid, public assistance grants, retired pay for government employees both military and civilian, agricultural price supports, the interstate highway program, and so on.

Thus, under present law it is almost futile to perform benefit/cost analysis or similar evaluations which may demonstrate that the government obtains a lower return on its investments in highway transportation than in air transportation or in some other alternative and, hence, that some shifting of funds might improve the national welfare. The futility arises from the simple fact that the highway programs are funded by taxes which basic legislation has earmarked for that purpose. Even in the presence of the most convincing analysis, the Congress cannot, through the annual budget process, transfer funds from surface to air transportation by reducing the appropriations for the Bureau of Public Roads and increasing those for the Federal Aviation Agency, even though both are units of the Department of Transportation.[2] The waters may have been muddied recently by the controversy over the President's use of the impoundment power, but the basic situation remains unchanged. The excise tax collections which are deposited in the highway fund cannot—under existing law—be used for another purpose, and no Chief Executive has ever attempted to do so.

Similarly, there is no discretion through the budget process to shift funds from an income-maintenance program such as public assistance to a human-resource investment activity such as education, although both are functions of the Department of Health, Education, and Welfare. This rigidity arises because the expenditures under the public assistance program are in the nature of fixed charges; they are predetermined by statutory formulas governing federal matching of state disbursements for welfare. Prior changes in the basic statute would be necessary in order to redirect the federal spending in this area.

There are many other examples of these institutional obstacles to improving the allocation of public resources, such as the continuation funding of an ongoing public works project (what is the value of half a bridge?). The end result of course is that the very process of public resource allocation itself is hardly that deliberate and systematic choice among alternatives that we economists like to envision in our analyses. This leads us to the second barrier to more rational decision-making on government spending—the fragmentation of congressional action on budget and fiscal matters.

Numerous shortcomings have been identified in the manner in which the Congress acts on the budget, ranging from lack of a formal computerized information system to the proliferation of uncoordinated committees and subcommittees that are involved in one or another stage of the process. Yet one shortcoming may be overriding—the lack of any means or mechanism for relating the numerous actions on specific pieces of legislation to the central issues of budget policy and national priorities.

When the rather substantial literature on budget reform is examined—and it is substantial —one is struck by the almost total emphasis on the preparation of the budget for submission to the Congress. Performance budgeting, program budgeting, benefit/cost analysis, cost/effectiveness evaluations—all these ambitious attempts at systematic analysis of budgetary proposals are basically designed for the executive branch of the government. Certainly, the presidential budget process has undergone fundamental change and improvement in the half-century since the passage of the historic Budget and Accounting Act of 1921.

In contrast, the congressional procedures are rather much the same as they were in the 1920s. Two very traditional proposals are consistently suggested for improving the legislative budget process—expenditure ceilings and omnibus appropriation bills. Both of them already have been attempted and with little or no success. Yet continually, almost yearly, these proposals are presented as brand new innovations.

But we need to recall that twenty-seven years ago the Legislative Reorganization Act of 1946 created a joint committee charged with recommending a ceiling on total expenditures to serve as a control on the amount of appropriations to be enacted. The legislative budget approach was tried in 1947 and again in 1948, and again in 1949. For a variety of reasons, it was abandoned; the ceiling was to be developed by a most unwieldy joint committee; the ceiling was established too late in the budget cycle to have much of an impact on the appropriations process; the procedure lacked any "teeth" in the face of breaches of the ceiling by individual committees of the Congress.

The second standard suggestion is to incorporate the traditionally separate appropriation measures into a one-package or omnibus appropriation bill. This obviously is an effort to get the Congress to act from the viewpoint of the total budget. After some prodding by the Senate in 1949, the House Appropriations Committee did voluntarily adopt such a procedure for all civilian appropriations for the fiscal year 1951. The experiment was not repeated. For one thing, this approach precluded the Senate from starting formal work on appropriation items until all of them were approved by the House. In practice, the omnibus bill was little more than a pasting together of the traditional individual appropriation bills. Also, the omnibus bill lent itself to the addition of legislative riders. As a practical matter, the President could not have prevented the riders which he deemed objectionable unless he were willing to veto the entire omnibus bill and thus delay (except for temporary continuing appropriations) the financing of all government agencies.

By and large, other proposals for congressional reforms have failed to gain even this amount of support because, basically, they would have required some members or committees to yield a portion of their prerogatives and powers. In part, of course, the reluctance to share congressional power more widely may have been ultimately self-defeating. Given the inability of the Congress as a whole to face the key issues of budget policy, the Chief Executive, perhaps inevitably, has come to exercise increasing control over the size and composition of government spending.

Yet, a broader historical perspective does show that the Congress repeatedly has changed the manner in which it organizes for and takes action on budgetary matters. In a sense, there has been a recurring ebb and flow of forces which shift from centralizing decision-making at one time to fragmentizing the process in another period. We may have reached a point where the ebb tide of congressional power is about to start the long process of reversal.

The Congress, of course, has not been oblivious to its own shortcomings. The Senate Finance Committee, in its report last year on the proposed expenditure ceiling, lamented that "in a period of strong, competing concepts of program priorities, all are accepted rather than choices among them being made."

The third key obstacle to a more rational allocation of public resources is the lack of a formal mechanism for making choices among alternative priorities. In a very real sense, the process is one of "bottom-up" decision-making. It is only when we add up the various appropriations for investment in human resources—education outlays in the Department of Health, Education, and Welfare, the National Science Foundation, and the Veterans Administration; manpower training in the Departments of Labor, Interior, and Housing and Urban Development; and medical activities in the Departments of Agriculture, Defense, and Health, Education, and Welfare—that we find out how great a portion of our resources is being devoted to this strategic area.

Of course, if we want to take that vital next step in any intelligent priority analysis—to find out what portion of our resources is being devoted to an alternative area of government spending, such as investments in physical resources—we have to go through the same laborious process. It is not the tedium of having to identify the bits and pieces of hundreds of different agencies and appropriations that is the basic problem. Rather, it is the knowledge that the decisions are being made piecemeal and in isolation. Hence, any aggregations that we may see—even those in the presidential budget—are usually made after the fact and not as part of the decision-making process.

Thus we may inquire as to why we are spending over $5 billion for highways and not much more than one-tenth of that amount ($652 million) for mass transportation; why we are spending twice as much on dams and other conventional Corps of Engineers and Bureau of Reclamation projects ($3.2 billion) than on pollution control and related environmental improvements ($1.6 billion); why we are spending $76 billion for the Department of Defense and only $10 million on the Arms Control and Disarmament Agency; why we are spending more for the programs specifically benefiting the 26 percent of the population living in rural areas ($5.7 billion in aid to farmers and rural development) than on the programs designed for the other 74 percent ($3.7 billion for housing and community facilities).

In raising these points I do not mean really to intrude my own personal value judgments. Rather I want to indicate the kinds of questions that do not even get raised in the budget process under present procedures but which so badly need our attention.

At least until recently, I would have added a fourth major obstacle to improving the situation— the absence of a sustained interest in and concern with these questions by the public or their legislative representatives or the leading communications media. Both dissatisfaction with the existing decision-making process and interest in improving it are now commonly and openly expressed by the very leadership of the Congress itself. This was clearly manifested in the establishment of a Joint Study Committee on Budget Control consisting not of young Turks without seniority but of chairmen or ranking members of the Appropriations, Ways and Means, and Finance Committees.

In its first report, the committee stated simply that the basic problem with which it is concerned is "the lack of congressional control over the budget." [3] It went on to state that the present institutional arrangements often "make it impossible to decide between competing priorities with the result that spending is made available for many programs where the preference might have been to make choices and also spending reductions." It is hardly the originality of these observations which I find so striking, but their source.

Because of the apparent basic change in this fourth and final category, the battered ranks of budget reformers have been strengthened recently. Courage has been summoned for literally another march up the hill (in a manner of speaking, Capitol Hill). Hence, let us examine some possibilities for change and improvement.

Some Possible Improvements

I am convinced that in these basic matters of public policy there are no ultimate solutions, in the sense of answers that are correct for all times and under varying circumstances. In that spirit, I would like to match each of the three obstacles that I have identified with a possible change, not a cure but hopefully an improvement.

In the case of the uncontrollable programs, the basic solution is quite evident—to make them subject to effective control in the annual budget and appropriations process, to enable both the presidential budget office and the congressional appropriations committees to begin their yearly work on the budget with a relatively clean slate. But upon closer examination, that suggestion has the characteristic of many good ideas: it will carry us only part of the way; it really cannot be pushed too far. That is, it would make very good sense to restore annual budget controllability to some of the privileged programs, such as the appropriation in the Department of Agriculture for the removal of surplus farm commodities.

At the present time, an amount equal to 40 percent of annual customs duties is automatically appropriated for agricultural subsidies. Clearly, the size of the resultant uncontrollable appropriation bears little if any relationship to the need of the program being financed, nor does it lend itself to being related to changing national priorities between agriculture and other areas of the society. The sensible thing to do in this case would be to terminate the special pipeline to the Treasury and require the program to be financed via appropriations which are voted on by the Congress each year.

Similarly, the expenditures on the program of federal aid to highways should not depend on the amounts collected from the sale of gasoline, tires, and other so-called highway-related excise taxes. Rather, the Congress should determine the relative priority to be assigned to highways in the budget and then appropriate the sums required. The result in a given year might well exceed the collections of the designated excises, or it might fall below.

There are many other "uncontrollable" programs and activities that should be stripped of their fiscal privileges. Yet, we must acknowledge that there are compelling reasons for not subjecting all government spending programs to the extended annual review. Interest on the public debt is the clearest example. Given the amount of and the composition of the Treasury's outstanding debt at any given point in time, there is no feasible alternative to paying the interest charges as they fall due. Should Congress attempt to convert the present permanent indefinite appropriation to an annual definite item, the result would at best be a good deal of wasted motion.

If the annual appropriation for interest turned out to be higher than necessary to service the public debt in a given year, the excess amount could not be spent. But if the funds appropriated turned out to be insufficient to cover the interest due and payable, the Congress would have to rush through a supplemental appropriation in order to avoid the embarrassment of the government defaulting on its own securities—aside from the adverse psychological repercussions on money markets and investor attitudes at home and abroad.

Clearly, some governmental activities are "naturally" uncontrollable within the confines of the annual budget process; such requirements in a very real sense are determined by exogenous factors. Until or unless the statutes creating these requirements are modified, they simply need to be allowed for in devising the government's fiscal plans. But the great many "artificially" uncontrollable programs—those determined by endogenous factors, within the purview of the Congress itself —need to be converted to fully controllable and budgetable items.

A related problem is the "backdoor financing" of many government undertakings. At the present time, many programs circumvent the appropriations process entirely. The same bill that authorizes the program often also provides the financing. This frequently has been done in such areas as housing and agriculture. A variety of transparent subterfuges has been used for avoiding formal appropriations, such as the so-called authorization to spend public debt receipts. Those authorizations require the Treasury to make disbursements in the same fashion as appropriations. The key difference of course is that the authority is not contained in an appropriations bill. Those programs do not have to be justified to the appropriations committees but only to what often are more sympathetic subject matter committees.

It is precisely such "backdoor financing" which makes so difficult the congressional determination of spending priorities. These special privileged pipelines to the Treasury also should be abandoned for direct appropriations.

A Budget Scorecard for the Congress

With reference to the need to relate the myriad of individual program decisions to the overall budget totals, there is a desirable reform that could be instituted quite quickly and perhaps without raising the objections usually encountered by the two substantive proposals of spending ceilings and omnibus appropriation bills. Without waiting until it adopts more basic reforms, the Congress should utilize the device of a "budget scorecard." Such a scorecard would show currently the effect of individual budget decisions on the overall state of federal finances.[4] To be sure, this is a far more modest change and hardly in the nature of a complete solution—which is why it may be more readily undertaken.

This approach differs from most of the other suggestions for budgetary reforms which have been offered in that it would not alter the internal distribution of power inherent in the existing organizational structure of the Congress or the way in which actions are taken on individual bills. Rather, the scorecard would be an analytical mechanism. It could be used by the existing committees of the Congress as they pursue existing appropriation procedures as well as by individual members as they participate in debates on the floor of the Congress.

It is the kind of statistical information that every baseball and football fan expects and receives at the ball park. In the case of the budget, neither the fans nor the players know whose winning or literally who's on first. An electronic budget scorecard should be prominently displayed in every congressional committee room as well as on the floor of the House and the Senate. Such a mechanism would enable each congressional body reviewing a given item to treat it as the marginal case. But it would merely be an informational aid to the members, rather than any dictum from on high. Table 1 contains such an illustrative budgetary scorecard. Several assumptions have been made in filling out the hypothetical scorecard:

Table 1

ILLUSTRATIVE BUDGETARY SCORECARD

| | 1973 (Current Year) | | 1974 (Budget Year) | | 1975 (Following Year) | |
	Presidential Submission	Current Estimate	Presidential Submission	Current Estimate	Presidential Submission	Current Estimate
Unified Budget Totals (in billions of dollars)						
Receipts	225	228	256	254	290	282
Outlays	250	255	269	272	288	294
	—	—	—	—	—	—

Surplus (+) Deficit (−)	−25	−27	−13	−18	+2	−12
Item Under Consideration (in millions of dollars)						
Appropriation for Air Force Procurement of Missiles						
Amount being considered:						
Expenditures	1452	1552	1582	1682	1680	1780
(Appropriations)	(1670)	(1670)	(1573)	(1773)	(1770)	(1880)

Note: Increased deficit will require higher taxes or larger public debt.

(1) That some congressional committee or staff—a point to which we will return—has supplied the revisions from the original presidential estimates.

(2) That the estimated deficit for the budget year (1974) has been increased through more liberal congressional action on previous items; the scorecard of course would work just as well if the case were the reverse.

Hopefully, the type of information in Table 1 would show the congressional committee acting on the proposed appropriation for the procurement of aircraft that (1) revenues are estimated to come in more slowly than projected in the budget, (2) congressional action to date has increased the prospective deficits by a more liberal attitude on expenditures, and (3) the specific item under consideration, if enacted at the currently recommended level, would raise the budget deficit for 1974 further still; moreover, (4) the surplus that the Administration has targeted for the following year is not likely to be achieved.

It is problematical whether the presentation of such data would, in fact, have any influence upon the deliberations of individual committees or the votes of individual members of the Congress. It would, nevertheless, provide a simple technique and substantiating figures for specific members of these and other committees who desired some analytical support for their positions.

At the least, the scorecard would be a means of appraising the effects of each individual fiscal action on the total budget outcome.

The scorecard could be used in conjunction with actions on a variety of bills—program authorizations, appropriations, and tax measures. Hence, it would maintain constantly for the attention of the Congress a recording of the ebb and flow of the current status of the budget picture for the ensuing fiscal year. The scorecard would contain a continuous updating of these figures, taking account of congressional action as well as changes in the economic outlook. The trend of congressional actions toward a higher level of spending (and a resultant larger deficit) would be revealed during rather than after the completion of the decision-making process.

The scorecard approach, by itself, would be politically neutral. It could be used extensively at the present time by those concerned with minimizing the federal deficit and thus dampening down inflationary pressures. It also could be used in different circumstances by advocates of a larger public sector to show that increases in spending should be made at a more rapid rate. This particularly could be the case in a recessionary period where greater amounts of fiscal stimulus are desired.

Use of the scorecard idea would require the services of staff personnel of congressional committees and/or administrative agencies to do the bookkeeping and to develop estimates of effects on expenditure or revenue figures of individual actions changing proposed new appropriations or affecting anticipated revenues. The term appropriations is here used in its broadest sense, meaning actions which permit government agencies to obligate the government to make expenditures. Technically, contract authorizations and authorizations to expend from public debt receipts are also included. This type of information readily lends itself to being programmed on even the most modest computer system for ready retrieval and updating.

The current reporting of budgetary action should not be limited to pending action by the appropriations and tax-writing committees. It should also be utilized by the substantive committees considering basic program legislation: agriculture, commerce, education, and so on. Thus, the birth stage of government spending programs, now often relatively immune from budgetary considerations, would be exposed to the type of financial concerns currently shared mainly by the appropriations and revenue committees.

The scorecard could be maintained by the staffs, possibly augmented, of the appropriations committees of each chamber. Alternatively, the task could be assigned to a new joint committee on the budget, should the Congress decide to

establish one. Another possibility would be to
build on the far more aggregated Scorekeeping
Report issued from time to time by the Joint Committee on Reduction of Federal Expenditures.[5]
Presumably, the revenue estimates would continue, as at present, to be prepared by the staff of
the Joint Committee on Internal Revenue Taxation, but their use would extend beyond the tax-
writing committees. Indeed the fine group of
career personnel that comprises the Joint Committee should serve as a prototype for the expenditure work that is envisioned in this proposal.

Alternatively, or in addition, the capabilities
of the General Accounting Office might be more
fully developed and drawn upon. This is a congressional, rather than an executive, agency which
has increased the scope and caliber of its analytical work very significantly during the last several years.

Whatever staff is assigned the task would
need to keep abreast of the actions of the various
substantive committees which provide financial
authorization for future federal spending. Also,
the working relationships would have to be developed so that the scorecards, when properly
prepared and made available, would actually be
utilized by the individual members of the Congress and in the deliberations of the various committees.

The third proposal that completes my triad of

recommended budgetary innovations is in the form of a rudimentary methodology for making decisions on priorities. It attempts to deal with what may be the most fundamental analytical shortcoming in the entire budget process—the failure to treat the budget process as a series of choices among alternatives.

Would an added dollar be more wisely spent for education or for highways? For job training or for income maintenance? These fundamental questions are not even raised in the budgetary process at the present time, much less are any answers sought. The current emphasis rather is on deciding whether to increase or decrease the funds to be allotted to the specific programs within each of these categories. Furthermore, the choices are usually restricted to those which can be made within each of the many agencies involved in education or income maintenance or any other specific functional areas. The notion of the need for or even the possibility of making a choice between an "income strategy" and an "investment strategy" does not even get recognized under present arrangements. Neither does the need to choose between added investments in human resources and in physical resources.

What is needed is a program budget for the entire federal government. Such a government-wide programmatic analysis would permit, if not require, decision-makers to compare alternative programs of different agencies which may contribute to achieving a given basic national goal. Hence, I would base such a budget on the fundamental objectives for which the various government programs are carried on. Merely for purpose of illustration, I have identified four such basic end purposes.

In a world of continuing international tensions, the initial purpose that comes to mind is the protection of the nation against external aggression—to maintain the national security. A variety of federal programs exists in this category, ranging from our own military establishment to bolstering the armed forces of other nations and to negotiating arms control agreements.

A second basic national purpose, one also going back to the Constitution, is the promotion of the public welfare. Here we find the federal government operating in the fields of Social Security, unemployment compensation, veterans pensions, and many other such income-maintenance and income-redistribution activities.

A third major purpose of government programs has received an increasing amount of attention in recent years: the necessary investments in the further development of the American economy. This area covers the various programs to develop our natural resources and transportation facilities, as well as support of education, health, research and development, and other efforts to increase economic growth. Finally, there is the routine day-to-day operation of the government itself, such as the functioning of the Congress and the courts, the collection of revenue, and the conduct of foreign relations.

Let us reconstruct the federal budget in this framework and thus see for ourselves what the implicit priorities really are. The key term of course is implicit. When we examine the budget and appropriation hearings over the years, we find little if any systematic attempt to appraise the wisdom or desirability of these overall choices in the allocation of government resources. Some of the results of such a reconstruction of the budget are clear. Public welfare, rather than national security, receives by far the largest share of the budget. At the present time the respective portions are two-fifths versus one-third. To be sure, the precise numbers have been influenced by the end of the Vietnam War. Yet, when we attempt to develop the data for a decade earlier, we find the same dominance of welfare over warfare.[6]

What may be more surprising, and may also be disconcerting to some, is the overwhelming dominance of civilian spending by income-maintenance or income-redistribution expenditures over investment outlays. A comparatively puny portion, about 13 percent of the total budget, is comprised of the various economic development efforts. That is, the bulk of civilian spending is devoted not to increasing the size of the nation's income pie but to rearranging the slices. This may come as a pleasant surprise to those analysts who recently have developed an interest in the possibilities of using government as a mechanism for redistributing income in our society. The fact of the matter is that a good deal of such activity is currently being performed; some may even contend that it already is excessive.

It is mere conjecture, of course, to wonder to what extent the allocation of government funds would have been different if the individual appropriation requests had been developed and reviewed in the overall context of priority decisions such as presented here. We can gain some added insight to the possible program choices that can and might be made in using this type of budgetary framework by making a somewhat deeper analysis of the content of each of the four categories (see Table 2).

As would be expected, the great bulk of the national security budget is devoted to the U.S. military forces. However, a little over one-tenth of the total is comprised of programs that would promote the national security through other means. This programmatic approach thus lends itself to raising and answering questions such as the following: Would national security be improved by shifting some of the $6.1 billion of foreign aid to our own military establishment?

Conversely, would the national security be strengthened by moving a proportionately small share of the direct military budget, say $200 million, to the U.S. Information Agency or to the arms control effort and thereby obtaining disproportionately large increases in these programs?

Also this level of detail permits some cross-comparisons of government programs which are not now made. For example, the $4.4 billion of foreign economic aid far exceeds the $2.7 billion devoted to the formal domestic antipoverty efforts. Would some trade-off between the public welfare and the national security areas result in a net advantage to the nation? This type of analysis is thus an attempt to raise in a quantitative manner the fundamental question, Would an extra dollar (a billion in the case of the federal government) be more wisely spent for program A or for program B? The very existence of the kind of information discussed here may lead not only to attempts to answer questions such as these, but, even more fundamentally, it would widen the horizon of budget reviewers, both in the executive branch and in the Congress.

A brief examination of the composition of the Economic Development category is revealing. Transportation facilities—mainly highways—account for the largest single share. When combined with natural resource development and business

Table 2
Table 2 (*continued*)
HYPOTHETICAL
GOVERNMENT-WIDE PROGRAM BUDGET
Fiscal Year 1973. (In billions of dollars)

Category	*Amount*
National Security	
U.S. military forces	82.4
Foreign economic aid	4.4
Scientific competition	3.4
Foreign military aid	1.7
Psychological competition	0.3
Total	92.2
Public Welfare	
Social insurance and retirement	60.8
Health services	20.1
Veterans' benefits	12.4
Public assistance	11.0
Aid to farmers and rural development	5.7
Housing and community facilities	3.7
Antipoverty programs	2.7
Specialized welfare activities	2.5
Total	118.9
Economic Development	
Transportation facilities	10.4
Education and research	8.0
Natural resources and regional development	6.3
Manpower development	4.4

Category	Amount
Health research and development	3.6
Business aids and subsidies	1.3
Total	34.0
General Government	
Interest on debt	21.2
General aid to states and localities	5.3
Government operations	3.7
Judicial and law enforcement	2.1
Foreign reltaions	.5
Intragovernmental transactions	−7.1
Total	25.7
Grand Total	270.8

subsidies, these investments in our physical resources come to 53 percent of the entire Economic Development category. Education, manpower training, and other investments in human resources receive the remaining 47 percent. A government-wide program budget could focus attention on questions such as, Would a shift of funds from physical to human resources be advisable? From highways to job training? Raising these questions need not be taken as expressions of value judgments, although one may wonder why highways have become our chosen national instrument for fostering economic growth and development. The point of course is to create new patterns of governmental decision-making in an effort to identify the areas of government spending that could yield greater returns to the nation and its taxpayers—as well as those areas that yield smaller returns on our national investment.

If this sort of analysis were incorporated into the annual budget document, it could result in growing congressional and public concern and awareness of the problems of choosing among alternative uses of government funds. In the absence of an automatic market mechanism, such an approach might introduce a healthy degree of competition among spending programs in the governmental resource-allocation process.

If the executive branch does not choose to take the initiative, then a congressional staff could rework the existing budget submissions within this framework for use by the entire appropriations committee in each House prior to its detailed examination of individual appropriation requests. Clearly, this would be a possible method of restoring some congressional leadership on budget matters. This approach would enable the appropriations committees to set general guidelines and ground rules for the detailed budgetary review by their subcommittees. It would also permit some improvement over the current situation, in which overall government policy often seems to be the accidental by-product of unrelated budget decisions on the various department requests, rather than the guiding hand behind those decisions.

It would be a great advantage if the subcommittee structure of the appropriations committees would be reorganized to conform more closely to program lines. The prospect of an effective, coordinated review is diminished by preserving a subcommittee structure which is patterned after department and agency lines which have been, or are, in the process of being abandoned.

Perhaps more basic, however, is the need to strengthen the role of the House Appropriations Committee vis-à-vis its individual subcommittees. At the present time, the parent committee often resembles a loose confederation or holding company of autonomous individual components. If the previous suggestions for strengthening the overall power of the committee are adopted, it would become even more important to make the subcommittees more responsive to the will and broader outlook of the full committee and thus of the Congress itself.

The underlying theme of this program approach to governmental budgeting is the need to array the alternatives so that deliberate choices can be made among them. This does not necessarily require the invention of very sophisticated methodology. It has its counterparts in the private sector. Many families rush out and spend the

Christmas bonus on a new car. A more prudent family may carefully, although subjectively, consider the relative benefits of a new car, a long summer vacation, or remodeling the basement. Similarly, a well-managed company would not impulsively decide to devote an increase in earnings to raising the dividend rate. Rather, it would carefully consider the alternative uses of the funds —embarking on a new research program, rebuilding an obsolescent manufacturing plant, or developing a new overseas operation. The basic requirement is the ability to make choices among alternatives, each of which seems attractive in its own right. But is that not a basic function of management, public or private?

Extensions of the Analysis

Any analysis of governmental priorities is inherently limited to the items which are contained in the budget itself. At present, two major types of governmental activities are not included in the budget proper. This substantially reduces the effectiveness of the entire budget process, particularly in the ability of both the President and the Congress to direct and influence the allocation of public resources in accordance with changing national priorities. Let us identify these activities and try to incorporate them into the analysis.

The first category of items omitted from the federal budget consists of uses of the credit of the federal government. The bulk of the lending which is supported and assisted by the federal government is now financed outside of the budget, and this trend is continuing. This is accomplished by means of various loan guarantee techniques and loans made by federally sponsored but ostensibly privately owned agencies, such as Federal National Mortgage Association (Fanny Mae) and the Federal Land Banks.

None of the $26.9 billion expansion in outstanding federal loans during the fiscal year 1974 is expected to be in the form of direct loans which show up in the budget. The increase consists entirely of so-called federally assisted credit programs which are outside of the budget and the budgeting process. There is slight government control over their expansion. Hence little consideration is given to their impacts on financial markets and on the overall economy.

The largest single category of federally assisted private credit is to the home mortgage market. This is accomplished through a variety of mechanisms, such as the Federal Housing Administration and the Veterans Administration guaranteeing home mortgages, the Fanny Mae providing a secondary market for VA and FHA mortgage lenders, and more recently the Federal Home Loan Bank System establishing a secondary market for conventional mortgages.

Despite the restraint that the Nixon Administration is currently exercising over budget expenditures, the size and variety of these extra-budgetary credit agencies are continuing to grow without interruption. To the old standbys of the farm and housing credit areas, the last few years have witnessed such creations as the Emergency Loan Guarantee Board (whose sole recipient is the Lockheed Aircraft Corporation), the Washington Metropolitan Area Transit Authority (whose bonds are guaranteed by the U.S. government), and the Student Loan Marketing Association. The latter, already nicknamed Sally Mae, is destined to serve as the Fanny Mae—providing a secondary market—for lending to college students.

So long as federally assisted loans and loan guarantees are excluded from the budget and thus are not subject to effective control by either the legislative or executive branches, there will be strong incentives to convert government spending from direct budget loans to these more indirect techniques. Perhaps the most flagrant case is that of the Export-Import Bank. That agency's operations were moved "outside" of the budget by the Congress, even though the bank is still a wholly federally owned enterprise and its debt issues are included along with those of the Treasury itself in the compilations of total borrowing and indebtedness of the federal government.

Clearly, any comprehensive analysis of governmental priorities needs to take account of the operation of these federally assisted credit programs. They can strongly influence the allocation of credit in the economy and, hence, the distribution of real resources, thus adding to the economic impact which is implied from an examination limited to the budget proper.

One way of integrating them into the budget process is to provide some control over their borrowing or lending. For example, Congress could impose a ceiling on the total borrowing of federal and federally sponsored credit agencies, both those "in" and those "out" of the budget, thus restricting the amount of funds available to them for their lending activities. Also, a ceiling could be enacted on the overall volume of debt created under federal loan guarantees, most of which— directly or indirectly—are contingent liabilities on the federal treasury.

There is a second type of governmentally related activity which is not included in the budget. Special exemptions, deductions, and credits in our tax system affect the economy in ways that could be accomplished by government spending. For example, the expenditure side of the budget properly shows direct federal financial assistance for private medical care. However, nowhere in the budget is account taken of the $3 billion a year foregone by the tax system by reason of the deduction of medical expenses and the exclusion of sick pay.

Similarly, the natural resource agencies of the federal government, such as the Department of the Interior, dutifully record outlays for expenditure programs in that area. However, no mention is made of the $2 billion of assistance to natural resource industries which is granted each year through depletion allowances and other special tax provisions.

It would be extremely useful to quantify the expenditure equivalents of these tax provisions and to compare them with the direct expenditures and also credit aids extended by government instrumentalities to achieve the same general purpose. Tax aids are a very hidden type of subsidy. They have the outward appearance of involving no government costs. They are, in effect, netted out of receipts by the taxpayers themselves, so that taxes paid, and hence revenues collected by the government, are net after adjustment for tax concessions. However, there is a very real cost to the government in terms of foregone revenue and to the society as a whole in terms of the increased share of current national output available to the beneficiary of the particular tax aid.

In theory, government accounting could take account of the explicit inclusion of a noncash transaction such as tax aids. There is some precedent in business accounting practices. Sales discounts are explicitly measured, although, like tax aids, they are nonmonetary transactions.

The tax aid, as I believe it should be measured, is simply the difference between the tax actually paid and the tax that would be paid in the absence of the specific provision. The difference is solely the immediate revenue effect on the public sector and hence the immediate, direct income effect on the private sector. No induced or indirect effects are taken into account, although these could be significant—and offsetting—in some cases. I would offer a strong word of caution. There is a great and lamentable temptation to label each and every tax aid as an "unfair loophole." I would not jump to that conclusion without a good deal of additional information. As a general matter, I find the case rather persuasive that tax incentives often can result in a more effective private sector solution of some important national problem than direct expenditures.

For example, the tax assistance provided to private charities may be far less a burden on the federal treasury than the alternative of federal operation of hospitals and other services for the poor. In the case of church-related institutions, the tax system may be the only constitutional way of providing public support. However, I see no need to beg the question as to whether direct expenditures or tax aids are preferable in any given program area. My concern is a far more modest one: tax aids are one among many alternative uses of potential federal revenues, and any comprehensive analysis needs to take account of them.

Personally, I find it useful in evaluating governmental priorities to bring together the direct outlays of the federal government, the tax aids, and the various credit programs. I must admit to some reluctance to doing so for fear of adding the proverbial apples and oranges—although those do add up to pieces or pounds of fruit. In this case, they all add up in terms of dollars, but not necessarily in terms of equivalent economic impact. However, we need to recall that there are somewhat similar problems in assessing the effects on resource allocation arising from different types of direct government expenditures—purchases versus transfer payments versus expenditure subsidies. Despite the obvious shortcomings, the results of a total "summing up" are helpful in any comprehensive analysis of governmental priorities.

In a few cases, the extrabudgetary credit and tax aids rival the magnitude of the direct federal expenditures in that functional area. The leading example is community development and housing, where the tax and credit activities are several times the size of the budget outlays for that function. On reflection, that situation should be expected, in view of the fact that most homeowners receive the benefit of federal tax deductions and/or FHA or VA mortgage guarantees, while very few participate in the overt subsidy programs financed within the budget.

In the case of general aid to state and local governments, the annual cost to the Treasury of the new general revenue sharing program is roughly equal to what I call the old revenue sharing program—the taxes lost through exempting the interest on municipal bonds and allowing taxpayers to deduct state and local taxes. In other cases, such as national defense, space exploration, and general government, the direct outlays account for virtually all of the governmental activity in the program area.

Clearly, the implied ranking of priorities which is based on examining direct federal outlays is subject to considerable modification when account is taken of those related government activities which take the place of direct expenditure. The most dramatic upward movements occur, as would be expected, in the areas of housing and aid to state and local governments. In contrast, several major categories experience some diminution in implicit priority, notably health and education. Again, it is difficult to assume that the allocation of government funds would have been precisely the same if this broader type of information were available to decision-makers.

Conclusion

Even in an economy as rich and productive as ours, resources are limited. Claims on income and output must be balanced against the economy's capacity to produce. As always, priorities will be established, either by design or by default, to permit the satisfaction of some demands over others. But any enlightened attempt to reorder and establish priorities cannot take place until we possess a clearer understanding both of the existing general ordering of priorities and the ways in which possible choices can be made.

Reducing the uncontrollable portion of the budget, instituting a congressional budget scorecard, and developing a comprehensive government-wide program budget all would be valuable additions to the existing decision-making process. The pressure of competing demands and the need for making hard choices result in a process which is difficult enough without further complicating matters by archaic institutional structures or the absence of necessary analytical information. Hopefully, improvement in the quality of our information can lead to improvement in the quality of our decisions. The practical, if not measurable, payoffs are impressive: avoidance of a tax increase and greater citizen satisfaction with public undertakings.

At the present time, there appears to be a log jam in the development of public policy in the United States. On budget and many other domestic program matters, there is developing what almost amounts to a standstill between the President and the Congress. The current outlook is for a period characterized by difficult relationships between the legislative and executive branches of the federal government. This is a situation which makes ambitious new spending or tax initiatives unlikely. Cutbacks in government programs—or, usually more accurately, slowdowns in their growth rates—could well be the order of the day. Given the rapid expansion in the economy and the continued inflationary pressures, these budget results appear to be consistent with the current needs of economic policy.

Rather than attempting to exacerbate the tensions and difficulties present in executive legislative activities, I have endeavored to develop some relatively modest but forward looking changes that perhaps can lead the public and governmental debate to higher ground. These proposals are all designed to further the sentiment expressed by an earlier Moskowitz lecturer, one of the wisest men that I have ever had the privilege of working with. As Arthur Burns recently told the special congressional committee on budget control, "But Congress can preserve and strengthen its powers only be exercising them." [7]

When we look beyond the immediate scene, we can envision a time when—as a result of the success of the current economy efforts in reducing the base of the budget—some new expenditure initiatives, albeit of modest proportions, may become feasible within the confines of the revenue growth from existing taxes. The current reevaluations of the effectiveness of existing public undertakings may well result in identifying new approaches to dealing with the difficult social, economic, and ecological problems that still continue to afflict our society. Hopefully, those new priorities will be arrived at by intentional and informed choice, rather than through the usual process of historical accident.

NOTES

1. Murray L. Weidenbaum and Dan Larkins, *The Federal Budget for 1973* (Washington, American Enterprise Insttiute, 1972), p. 52.

2. See Murray L. Weidenbaum, "Institutional Obstacles to Reallocating Government Expenditures," in Robert Haveman and Julius Margolis, editors, *Public Expenditures and Policy Analysis* (Chicago, Markham, 1970), pp. 232-245.

3. U.S. Congress, Joint Study Committee on Budget Control, *Improving Congressional Control Over Budgetary Outlay and Receipt Totals* (Washington, U.S. Government Printing Office, 1973), p. 4.

4. For an earlier version, see Murray L. Weidenbaum, *Federal Budgeting: The Choice of Government Programs* (Washington, American Enterprise Institute, 1964), pp. 76-81.

5. See U.S. Congress, Joint Committee on Reduction of Federal Expenditures, *1973 Budget Scorekeeping Report*, Staff Report No. 9 (Washington, U.S. Government Printing Office, 1972).

6. See Murray L. Weidenbaum, *Federal Budgeting: The Choice of Government Programs* (Washington, American Enterprise Institute, 1964), pp. 59-69.

7. Statement by Arthur F. Burns, Chairman, Board of Governors of the Federal Researve System, before the Joint Study Committee on Budget Control, March 6, 1973, p. 13.

DISCUSSANT, MOSKOWITZ LECTURE

Lawrence S. Ritter

Professor of Finance
The Graduate School
of Business Administration
New York University

Although I greatly enjoyed both distinguished papers, I cannot help feeling that something essential is missing: like a performance of Hamlet without the prince or Macbeth without a murder.

Our overall theme today is "Fiscal Responsibility: Tax Increases or Spending Cuts?"—and yet on such a theme, at a conference held in the heart of New York City, we have heard virtually nothing about the issues that are uppermost in terms of priorities in the minds of so many Americans at this time and place. Namely, how can we arrest, and indeed reverse, the deterioration of our inner cities? How can we provide equal opportunity for the minorities that now inhabit those cities? How can we rid the nation's air and water of the pollution that threatens to engulf us all? How can we, in short, reorder our national priorities toward setting things in better order domestically now that the war in Southeast Asia no longer saps our energies abroad?

Professor Murray Weidenbaum's paper is titled "Government Expenditures and National Priorities," a subject on which Professor Weidenbaum has made numerous contributions over the past decade. No one has done more than he to bring logic and rationality to our budget-making procedures. His main point is indeed well taken: if a reordering of priorities is to mean ranking some priorities higher on the scale, then it simultaneously implies the other side of the coin— ranking some other things lower. This elementary logic is usually ignored by observers of all political persuasions, liberals and conservatives, radicals and reactionaries alike. The point is valuable and needs constant reiteration.

However, neither Professor Weidenbaum nor Professor McCracken have mentioned anything at all about the priorities *issues* that currently beset us. Our needs are distressingly clear: more equal opportunity for minority groups, better housing and health care for all, inner-city educational overhaul, reform of law enforcement and the judicial system, improved mass transit, and so on down what has become a rather familiar and all too lengthy list. Spending more money toward

these ends will not *in itself* accomplish anything
—we have learned *that* from the past four decades
—but without more spending as part of an overall effort the status quo is all too likely to remain
firmly entrenched.

To realize these priorities and to move them
higher up on the scale implies that other things
must be ranked lower. And yet isn't it ironic that
now, with the Vietnam War finally at an end, we
see an administration proposing to *increase* defense spending for the first time since 1969. We
are in the midst of the very cul-de-sac which Professor Weidenbaum has so cogently warned us
against: if *everything* is to be upgraded, including
military spending, then of course in the end
nothing will be upgraded and we will continue
along in the same old rut.

By their silence, Professors Weidenbaum and
McCracken indicate their agreement, or at least
their lack of serious disagreement, with our existing priorities. Indeed, Professor Weidenbaum
assures us that "public welfare," not "national defense," already receives the lion's share of the
budget. This shows, he says, the dominance of
"welfare over warfare." He should note, however,
that this use of the term "welfare" includes all
veterans' benefits, which are more war-related
than peace-related. And in any event, the great
bulk of "welfare" consists of Social Security benefits, which I have no intention of denigrating but

which we should realize are a response to the challenges of the 1930s, not the 1970s.

Regardless of such aggregates, when we turn to calculations on a *marginal* basis—to the shifting of funds from here to there—what we are seeing now is renewed emphasis on defense expenditures on the one hand but "fiscal responsibility" on the other. When funds are impounded by executive fiat, it is not military spending that is curtailed but antipollution spending. When the budget is trimmed, it is not the Pentagon that is cut back, but the Office of Economic Opportunity.

Major funding has been proposed in the coming year for the Trident submarine, for a new nuclear aircraft carrier, for seven new destroyers, and for seventy-seven new F-15 fighter planes. What I am saying, in a nutshell, is that in any discussion of government spending and national priorities we should at least raise the issue of submarines versus day-care centers, nuclear carriers versus better health care, destroyers versus less crime in the streets, fighter planes versus job training for the unemployed. And if we decide in each and every case that we do indeed want the military hardware, then we have to think about whether or not taxes should be raised to improve social services at the expense of private consumption.

Such choices, of course, involve value judgments, but isn't that precisely what national priorities are all about? Our current pattern of government spending is also shot through with value judgments, and it is a moot question whether it embodies the value judgments of a majority of the electorate or the vested interests of the powerful few. In any case, these are the issues I wish Professors Weidenbaum and McCracken had addressed themselves to. Lord knows, they are more important for the future of this country than flexible exchange rates or improved budget-making procedures—both of which, by the way, I heartily favor. It's just a matter of what's more important—in other words, a matter of priorities.

DISCUSSANT, MOSKOWITZ LECTURE

Robert A. Kavesh

Professor of Economics and Finance
The Graduate School
of Business Administration
New York University

Professors McCracken and Weidenbaum are illustrious members of the ranks of economists who have doffed their academic attire to do battle temporarily in the political arena and who have returned to the generally less controversial world of research, conjecture, and teaching. The nation owes them a great debt for their unselfish efforts in seeking ways to solve the unending and overwhelming problems that beset every administration, Republican or Democratic. Economists everywhere—of every shade of opinion and conviction—should be proud of the profession's past representation in Washington and of the generally good performance turned in under what must surely be considered "combat" circumstances.

At the risk of becoming too pedantic and reverting to my quizlike mentality, I suggest that an appropriate grade for the past work of economists in the Council of Economic Advisers and in the executive branches of government would be an average of B+. This may reflect my biased admiration for those willing to "dream the impossible dream"; it may also reflect the fact that I have a reputation as a very high grader.

Be that as it may, the theme of this conference, dealing as it does with issues such as "Government Expenditures and Tax Reforms" and "Fiscal Responsibility: Tax Increases or Spending Cuts?," is one that is replete with the opportunity for controversy. Honorable people may disagree —they inevitably do—when confronted with the set of problems incorporated in these topics. The methods, techniques, and analytical approaches used by economists of every political stripe are similar; the assumptions, data, and generalizations are where the differences of opinion crop up. So be it.

Professor McCracken has chosen a very broad canvas to paint. His particular subject "Foundations for Economic Policy in the 1970s" is reminiscent of Michelangelo's masterpiece in the Sistine Chapel, covering past, present and future—both good and evil—in glorious perspective.

One cannot disagree with many of the key points in Professor McCracken's analysis. He points up, and rightly, the growing dangers of isolationism and protectionism that threaten to rend the fabric of international cooperation. Neomercantilism is the greatest enemy of lasting world peace—and this is one of the few matters on which literally every economist agrees. On details and explanations, however, the focus of recrimination differs. I, for one, find it difficult to be sympathetic with the behavior of Japan in recent years, as that nation experienced an export upsurge unmatched by any other country. Their huge surpluses and their relative unwillingness to permit counterpart imports have complicated the task of expanding world trade with fragile liquidity instruments. Professor McCracken is more generous than I am prepared to be in asking us to understand the special problems of the Japanese. Frankly, I see their behavior as obdurate, shortsighted and ominous.

Another area of concern that Professor McCracken applies his brush to is the domestic economic scene. He ranges over the disappointments of the Vietnamese War years—that period that conjures up memories of the "seven bad years" prophesied so accurately by Joseph in biblical times. The details are familiar to all of us who agonized over this period. On again-off again shifts in monetary and fiscal policy, battling the Phillips Curve, the exporting to America of that uniquely British disease: stagflation—this is the sorry chronicle that plagued two Washington administrations—and, to a certain extent, it still does.

Professor McCracken surveys this record as a lesson of history and sees at least some cause for future optimism. In part this is relative; we stand a better chance of containing inflationary pressures than do the other major industrial nations. Small comfort, perhaps, but comfort nonetheless. Using this as a base he focuses upon the appropriate style of fiscal policy to ensure balanced growth without major inflationary pressures. Here he emphasizes the "full employment" balanced budget coupled with measures designed to help screen proposals; in a sense, a priorities system. And as an added feature he recommends that the President be granted "limited authority" to vary tax rates as a countercyclical measure. He recognizes, however, that the Congress may well take a jaundiced view of this latter suggestion.

A bold canvas, but yet an incomplete one. Where, for example, in all this discussion is there any mention of the tragic plight of the developing nations who, all too often, serve as pawns in the struggle among the giants? Surely something can —and must—be done to upgrade these economies as part of a worldwide effort to raise living standards.

And, coming closer to home, have we really done justice to the discussion of fiscal policy if the emphasis is placed solely on the question of how we can *cut* expenditures? To be sure, examples of waste and excesses in spending at all governmental levels abound, and one is on the side of the angels in urging a large-scale assault on many of these previously protected provinces of privilege.

But cutting may well be carried to excess. Absolute ceilings on total governmental outlays may elicit grass roots and (even) congressional support. Yet one small voice wonders if in the zeal to prune the dead branches we may well be carving deeply into the roots and trunk of the tree of state. In other words, perhaps we should be doing more to increase outlays in a variety of areas (medical research, environmental quality, poverty), areas integrally related to what we rarely talk about any more: the quality of life.

This, of course, gets us into the other side of the story: the story of governmental expenditures *and* receipts. Murmurs may follow about the present crushing burden of taxation and the impossibility of contemplating any further rise in assessments. Perhaps. But are we really sure that the present tax structure is as fair as it should be? Could we not institute some meaningful reforms in the system of taxation that would bring in more revenue and still not serve to stifle initiative and productivity? My own answers to these questions (and many more could be raised) are no to the first and yes to the second. Study after study confirms my judgment; isn't it about time that we took these issues seriously?

A mature reappraisal of the *entire* spectrum of fiscal policy would certainly help to provide the firm foundation for economic policy that Professor McCracken is so justifiably concerned about.